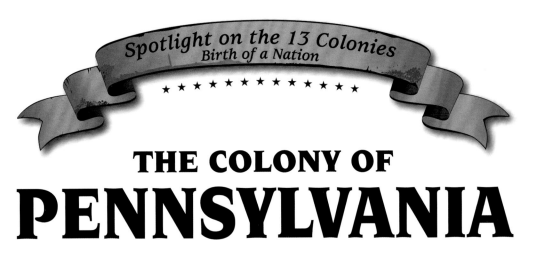

Spotlight on the 13 Colonies
Birth of a Nation

★ ★ ★ ★ ★ ★ ★ ★ ★ ★ ★ ★ ★ ★

THE COLONY OF
PENNSYLVANIA

David Martin

PowerKiDS press™

NEW YORK

Published in 2016 by The Rosen Publishing Group, Inc.
29 East 21st Street, New York, NY 10010

Editor: Sarah Machajewski
Book Design: Andrea Davison-Bartolotta

Photo Credits: Cover Edward Hicks/Getty Images; pp. 4–5 Delmas Lehman/Shutterstock.com; p. 6 Songquan Deng/Shutterstock.com; p. 7 Library of Congress/Wikimedia Commons; pp. 8–9 (main), 12–13 North Wind Picture Archive; p. 9 (inset) Courtesy of the Library of Congress; pp. 10–11 Stock Montage/Getty Images; p. 15 Ann Ronan Pictures/Print Collector/Getty Images; p. 17 trekandshoot/Shutterstock.com; p. 19 Hulton Archive/Getty Images; p. 21 UniversalImagesGroup/Getty Images; p. 22 VectorPic/Shutterstock.com.

Library of Congress Cataloging-in-Publication Data

Martin, David.
The colony of Pennsylvania / by David Martin.
p. cm. — (Spotlight on the 13 colonies: Birth of a nation)
Includes index.
ISBN 978-1-4994-0572-9 (pbk.)
ISBN 978-1-4994-0573-6 (6 pack)
ISBN 978-1-4994-0575-0 (library binding)
1. Pennsylvania — History — Colonial period, ca. 1600 – 1775 — Juvenile literature. 2. Pennsylvania — History — Revolution, 1775 – 1783 — Juvenile literature. I. Martin, David. II. Title.
F152.M38 2015
974.8/02—d23

Manufactured in the United States of America

CPSIA Compliance Information: Batch #WS15PK: For further information contact Rosen Publishing, New York, New York at 1-800-237-9932.

Contents

The First People of Pennsylvania

Pennsylvania's history began long before it became a state. It even began long before Europeans colonized it. **Ancestors** of Native Americans occupied the land that's now Pennsylvania anywhere from 12,000 to 18,000 years before the colony was founded. By the time Europeans arrived, several tribes were living around the future colony, including the Lenni Lenape (also known as the Delaware), Susquehannock, Shawnee, and Erie.

The first European to see Pennsylvania was Captain John Smith. He visited Pennsylvania during his exploration of the Chesapeake Bay from 1607 to 1609. The first Europeans to settle Pennsylvania were the Swedes. The Swedes already had established a colony in present-day Delaware, called New Sweden. They expanded into Pennsylvania in 1643 and built two forts on Tinicum Island. Explorers from other European nations, such as the Dutch, began trading with the Swedes in Pennsylvania as early as 1647. However, the Dutch and Swedes didn't get along, and the Dutch seized the Swedes' land in Pennsylvania in 1650. They kept it until 1664, when the British took control.

Pennsylvania is known for its beautiful geography. This image shows what early explorers, such as John Smith and French explorer Étienne Brûlé (who may have reached the upper-middle part of Pennsylvania between 1616 and 1618) may have seen when they reached present-day Pennsylvania.

Penn's Woods

The British controlled land that became Pennsylvania for almost 20 years before they officially colonized it. That happened in 1681, thanks to a man named William Penn.

William Penn was born in Britain. He was a Quaker, or a member of a group called the Religious Society of Friends. Penn—and the Quakers—believed in the idea of religious tolerance, which is the belief that people should be allowed to practice their religion freely. Many of the Quakers' beliefs were uncommon at the time, and Penn was jailed several times for **expressing** his beliefs.

Penn lived in Britain during the reign of Charles II. Under his rule, Britain wasn't a place of religious freedom. Penn felt people needed a place where they could practice their religion openly. He thought the American colonies would be a good place to start this kind of community. He called this plan the "holy experiment." In 1681, Charles II granted Penn a **charter** for land in North America. The land was named Pennsylvania, which means "Penn's Woods."

Charles II granted land to Penn to honor his father's service to Britain. Admiral Sir William Penn was an officer in the British navy who won many battles and land for Britain. He died in 1670, 11 years before William Penn received land in America.

Penn

Charles II

Progressive Pennsylvania

The charter for Pennsylvania became official on April 2, 1681. Penn named his cousin William Markham as Pennsylvania's deputy governor. Markham set out for North America, while Penn remained in Britain.

Penn's first task was to create a constitution, or set of laws. He named it the Frame of the Government of the **Province** of Pennsylvania. Penn wrote the constitution based on his beliefs. He said the colony would be a place of absolute religious freedom and that colonists had the right to an open discourse, which means they could share their ideas freely. The constitution limited Penn's power as a leader, created a two-house system of government, and protected colonists' property rights. Some of these ideas were influenced by Penn's **contemporary**, an important thinker named John Locke.

Penn also included a **clause** that said the constitution could be changed in the future based on the changing needs of the colonists. The Frame of the Government is viewed as **progressive** because its ideas were unlike those of other governments at the time.

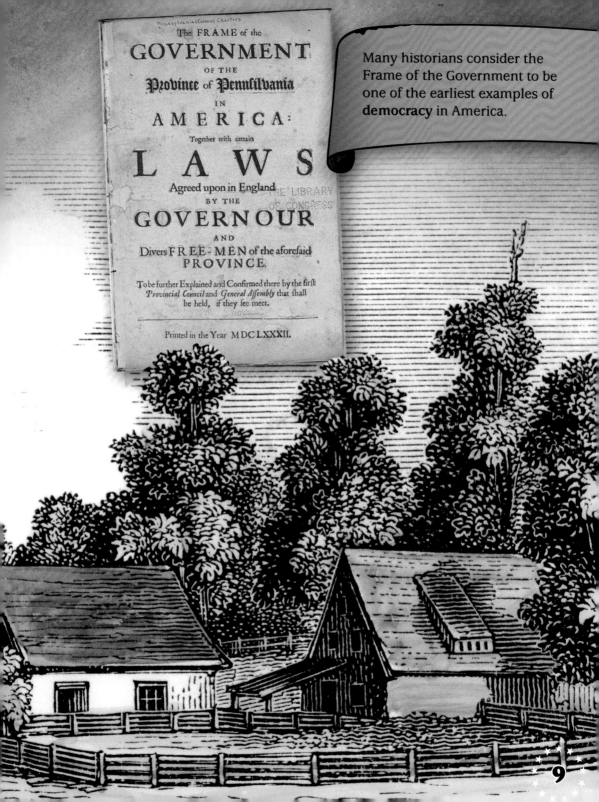

The FRAME of the
GOVERNMENT
OF THE
Province of Pennsilvania
IN
AMERICA:
Together with certain
LAWS
Agreed upon in England
BY THE
GOVERNOUR
AND
Divers FREE-MEN of the aforesaid
PROVINCE.

To be further Explained and Confirmed there by the first
Provincial Council and General Assembly that shall
be held, if they see meet.

Printed in the Year MDCLXXXII.

Many historians consider the Frame of the Government to be one of the earliest examples of **democracy** in America.

Penn Arrives in Pennsylvania

Penn set out for Pennsylvania in 1682. He and a group of Quakers sailed across the Atlantic Ocean on a ship called the *Welcome*. When he arrived, he found his "holy experiment" already underway. Many colonists had settled on the rich farmlands around the colony. A city named Philadelphia had been laid out according to plans Penn had made in Britain.

Penn planned Philadelphia to have wide main streets and small side streets, as well as plenty of open space for public use. The plan also allowed for growth in the future. Philadelphia was the first major American city to include these three features.

Even though Penn was granted land under Charles II's charter, the land actually belonged to the Native Americans living there. Penn chose not to occupy or settle it without buying it from the native people first. Penn met with the Lenni Lenape, Susquehannock, and Shawnee Indians, and established good relations with them. Buying their land—instead of taking it—was a sign of respect. This allowed both colonists and natives to live in peace.

This image shows Penn helping to lay out the streets of Philadelphia.

A Place of Many Cultures

In 1680, Pennsylvania's population of colonists was just under 700 people. The population increased to 11,450 by 1690. By the end of the colonial period in the late 1700s, the population was more than 327,000.

The Native American population decreased as European settlement increased. Most British settlers were Quakers, but many were **Anglican**. British colonists settled in the southeastern part of the colony, in and around Philadelphia. This helped Philadelphia become a **thriving** city.

German settlers were drawn to Pennsylvania, too. They made up almost a third of the colony's population by the late 1700s. They founded cities such as Lancaster and Germantown and helped grow Pennsylvania's farming **culture**.

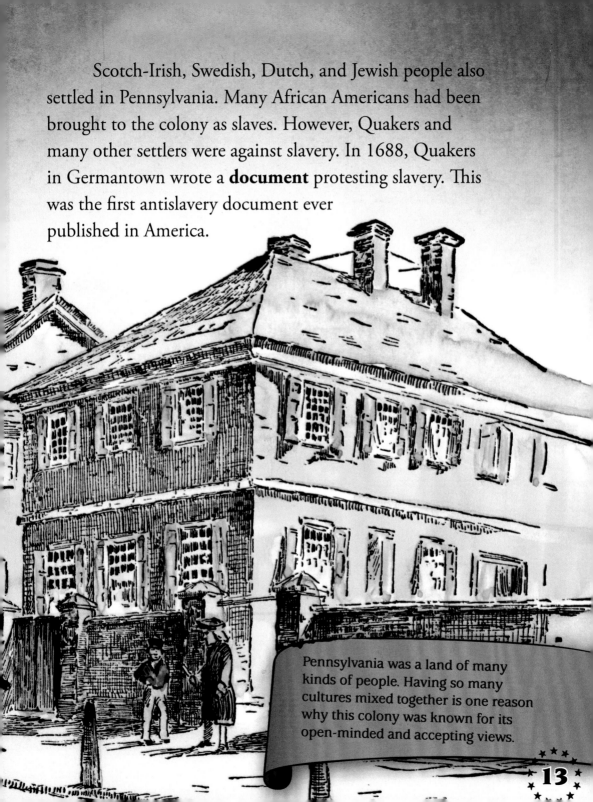

Scotch-Irish, Swedish, Dutch, and Jewish people also settled in Pennsylvania. Many African Americans had been brought to the colony as slaves. However, Quakers and many other settlers were against slavery. In 1688, Quakers in Germantown wrote a **document** protesting slavery. This was the first antislavery document ever published in America.

Pennsylvania was a land of many kinds of people. Having so many cultures mixed together is one reason why this colony was known for its open-minded and accepting views.

Government in Pennsylvania

William Penn stayed in Pennsylvania until 1684, when he sailed back to Britain. He stayed there for 15 years. He returned to Pennsylvania in October 1699. During this visit, he signed a document he had written called the Charter of Privileges. The charter made Pennsylvania the first American colony to have a democratic government.

Penn's charter stated that there should be a governing body run by colonists. He gave this governing body the power to make laws. The people had the power to elect **representatives**. He also **guaranteed** that colonists would have the same rights as other British citizens. Penn made sure to include the ideas of religious freedom and acceptance in his charter. He even made it okay for people of any Christian religion to be elected to the colony's government. One of the most important parts of the charter was that it said the government couldn't make somebody do something that went against their beliefs.

Penn left Pennsylvania after signing this document. He never returned to the colony, but the Charter of Privileges remained Pennsylvania's form of government until 1776.

Pennsylvania colonists had many freedoms. Here, they're seen meeting with Penn to discuss their ideas.

Life in the Colony

Pennsylvania was successful from the beginning. Many people decided to live in Pennsylvania because the colony's government had a land policy that attracted settlers. As more arrived, they started taking land that belonged to Native Americans. William Penn had made agreements with Pennsylvania's Indians that this wouldn't happen, but once he returned to Britain, there was no way to prevent these promises from being broken. This hurt the colonists' relationships with the native tribes in the area.

With its rich farmlands and growing cities, Pennsylvania held many economic opportunities for colonists. Wheat and corn were the colony's most important crops. Manufacturing was a big industry, since the colony had a wealth of **natural resources**. Cloth, iron, paper, and ships were all created in Pennsylvania.

One of the most important parts of Pennsylvania was Philadelphia. The city was a place of culture and learning. It had schools and libraries. Many famous Americans lived there, including Benjamin Franklin and Betsy Ross. Philadelphia was a key city throughout the American Revolution and became a center of government during and after the fight for independence.

This image shows Independence Hall in Philadelphia, which was once known as the Pennsylvania State House. It has been referred to as the "birthplace of the United States" because of the activity that took place there during the American Revolution.

Unrest in the American Colonies

Britain continued to form colonies until the 1730s. It wasn't the only country that wanted land, though. Britain and France fought over land in North America during the French and Indian War, which lasted from 1754 to 1763. Britain won, but the victory was expensive. Britain needed money to pay for the war. It also needed money to keep British soldiers in the colonies to maintain peace between colonists and Native Americans. The British government decided to raise money by taxing the colonists.

Britain taxed many kinds of goods, including tea and sugar. The Stamp Act of 1765 was a tax on every piece of paper the colonists used. These taxes made colonists very angry. Benjamin Franklin supported the Stamp Act at first. However, once he learned how other Pennsylvanians felt, he changed his mind. Franklin ran a newspaper called the *Pennsylvania Gazette*. He published stories that told people to fight the taxes. Some Pennsylvanians protested by joining a group called the Sons of Liberty. There were so many people against the tax that Britain ended the Stamp Act in 1766.

Britain's taxes made colonists angry because they had no say in whether or not they wanted to be taxed. The phrase "No taxation without representation" came to represent how colonists wanted to be governed.

Declaring Independence

Taxation was just one issue that made colonists unhappy with Britain. As the next 10 years passed, the idea of independence began to spread. Patriots were colonists who wanted independence. Loyalists were colonists who still wanted to be ruled by Britain.

Eventually, unhappiness with Britain became so strong that leaders from the colonies decided to meet and discuss what their issues were. In 1774, **delegates** from 12 colonies met in Carpenters' Hall in Philadelphia. Pennsylvania's delegates included Thomas Mifflin, who later became the first governor of Pennsylvania. These meetings have become known as the First Continental Congress.

Problems between the colonies and Britain continued to grow, and fighting broke out in April 1775 at Lexington and Concord in Massachusetts. These battles began the American Revolution. In May 1775, colonial representatives met again in Philadelphia to discuss what to do. These meetings, now known as the Second Continental Congress, took place in Independence Hall. A little over one year later, on July 4, 1776, the representatives approved the Declaration of Independence. Signing began on August 2. Benjamin Franklin was one important Pennsylvanian who signed this document.

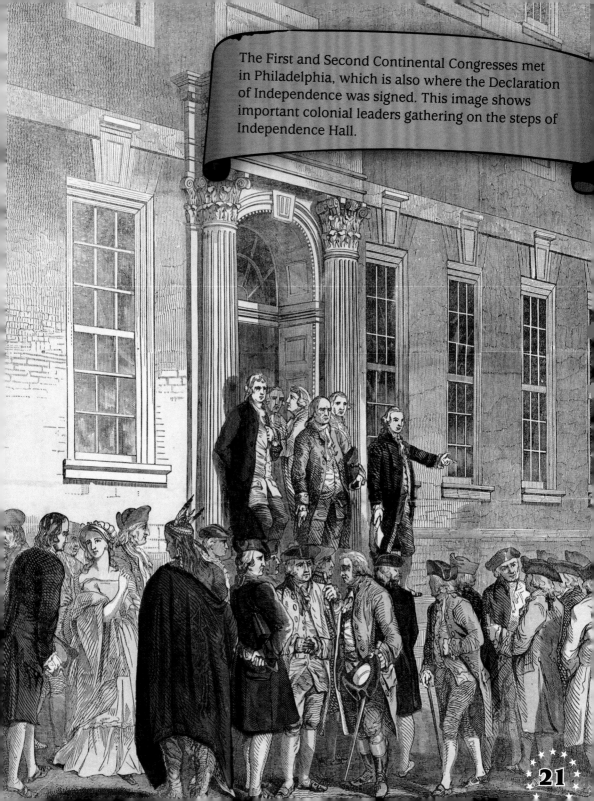

The First and Second Continental Congresses met in Philadelphia, which is also where the Declaration of Independence was signed. This image shows important colonial leaders gathering on the steps of Independence Hall.

The Second State

The Revolutionary War began in 1775. The fighting reached Pennsylvania in 1777 at the Battle of Brandywine. The British beat the Americans and occupied Philadelphia. Then, the Battle of Germantown occurred. After this battle, the Continental army, led by George Washington, camped out and trained in Valley Forge, Pennsylvania—just 20 miles (32 km) away. Though no fighting occurred at Valley Forge, it was a key place in the Revolutionary War because it was there that the Continental army trained and became stronger.

The war officially ended in 1783 with the signing of the Treaty of Paris. The new United States followed a set of laws called the Articles of Confederation. These laws weren't very successful. In 1787, representatives met in Philadelphia again to discuss the Articles of Confederation. Benjamin Franklin, Thomas Mifflin, and six other men represented Pennsylvania. The meeting resulted in a new set of laws called the Constitution. It's still used by the United States today. On December 12, 1787, representatives from Pennsylvania accepted the Constitution and it became the second state in the new nation.

Glossary

ancestor: A person who comes before others in their family tree.

Anglican: A member of the Church of England.

charter: A piece of writing from a king or other leader that grants or guarantees something.

clause: A separate section of a treaty, bill, or law that states something important.

contemporary: A person living at the same time as another.

culture: The ways of life of a group of people.

delegate: A person sent to a meeting or convention to represent others.

democracy: A political system in which the people hold power.

document: A piece of written matter that provides information or that serves as an official record.

express: To state.

guarantee: To make sure.

natural resource: Something in nature that helps people survive or that people can use to make things we need.

progressive: Ahead of its time.

province: An area of a country.

representative: Someone who is chosen to act or speak for other people.

thriving: Strong and successful.

Index

Primary Source List

Page 9 (inset). *The Frame of the Government of the Province of Pennsilvania in America, 1682.* Written by William Penn. Printed by William Bradford. Ink on paper. Created before 1689. Now kept in the Library of Congress Rare Book and Special Collections Division, Washington, D.C.

Page 17. Independence Hall. Designed by Edmund Woolley. Brick, marble, and wood. Built 1732–1756. Now located in Philadelphia, PA.

Websites

Due to the changing nature of Internet links, PowerKids Press has developed an online list of websites related to the subject of this book. This site is updated regularly. Please use this link to access the list: www.powerkidslinks.com/s13c/penn